The Pocket

OUTDOOR

SURVIVAL

GUIDE

The Ultimate Guide for Short-Term Survival

by J. Wayne Fears

Skyhorse Publishing

Skyhorse Publishing books may be purchased in bulk at special discounts for sales promotion, corporate gifts, fund-raising, or educational purposes. Special editions can also be created to specifications. For details, contact the Special Sales Department, Skyhorse Publishing, 307 West 36th Street, 11th Floor, New York, NY 10018 or info@skyhorsepublishing.com.

www.skyhorsepublishing.com

20 19 18 17 16 15 14 13

Library of Congress Cataloging-in-Publication Data

Fears, J. Wayne, 1938-
  The pocket outdoor survival guide : the ultimate guide for short-term survival / J. Wayne Fears.
       p. cm.
  ISBN 978-1-61608-050-1 (pbk. : alk. paper)
  1. Wilderness survival. 2. Outdoor life--Safety measures. I. Title.
  GV200.5.F46 2011
  613.6'9--dc22

                                        2010036070

Printed in China

PHOTOGRAPHY CREDITS
C.W. Brown/Photo Researchers, Inc. p.84
L. West/Photo Researchers, Inc. p.86
Scott Camazine/Photo Researchers, Inc. p.92
Alex Bowers p.113

*To those dedicated search & rescue
professionals and volunteers
who find countless lost and
stranded people each year.
Many lives would be lost
without them.
Thank you.*

TABLE OF CONTENTS

CHAPTER 4: WEATHER

CHAPTER 5: TROUBLE

CHAPTER 6: SIGNALS

CHAPTER 7: SHELTER

CHAPTER 8: BUILD A FIRE

CHAPTER 9: SLEEPING

CHAPTER 10: INSECTS

CHAPTER 11: SAFE WATER

CHAPTER 12: FOOD

CHAPTER 13: HYPOTHERMIA

CHAPTER 14: FEAR

CHAPTER 15: WILL TO LIVE

CHAPTER 16: MISSING PERSON

INTRODUCTION

Survival Is Usually an Unplanned Night in the Woods

Each year dozens of American outdoor enthusiasts find themselves in an unexpected outdoor emergency. They get lost, injured, or stranded and suddenly find themselves depending upon survival skills to survive. For most people, thanks to modern communications such as cell phones and two-way radios, it is merely a sobering two- or three-hour adventure. In fact, with today's methods of search and rescue, the majority of missing people are found within 72 hours after they have been reported missing, most even less. However, for some who do not take the proper precautions or do not have survival skills, such an experience can end in tragedy.

The purpose of this book is to help you prepare for that "unplanned night or nights in the woods." Keep it with you to help you make it through the adventure. With proper preparation for any outdoor activity, there should be little reason for an unplanned night in the woods. But, should you find yourself in a

North America still has lots of back-country in which it is easy to get lost or stranded. Even in the most remote country, however, most missing people are found within a few hours.

situation where you will need to survive several days, this book will have you prepared to do it with style. Survival knowledge and training pays off when the chips are down. Remember the acronym, "LOST"—Lean On Survival Training.

A sudden spill in a canoe can leave you stranded.

Survival Training Pays

Several years ago, when I was working as a wildlife manager in Georgia, I helped lead the search for a missing hunter in the rugged mountains along the Georgia-North Carolina boundary. We were told that this hunter had little hunting experience but had received extensive survival training. In a blinding rain-storm, it took us two days to find the lost hunter. Much to our surprise, by the time we found him he had virtually established a comfortable homestead.

When he first realized he was lost, he stopped walking and picked an opening in the dense woods to establish a survival camp. He immediately put out ground-to-air signals. Realizing bad weather was on the way, he built a shelter under some overhanging rocks that kept him dry and out of the wind. He gathered plenty of firewood and stored it in his shelter. Next, he built a fire complete with a reflector to keep his shelter warm.

It was his fire that led to his being found. The hunter's survival camp was so comfortable that those of us in the search party used it for an overnight rest before packing out.

When you first realize you are lost,
stop. Do not wander around aimlessly.
For every hour you wander the
search area grows four times.

Due to his survival training, he lived comfortably
through a two-day storm. He stayed positive and
worked toward being found. He used the
resources at hand to make a survival camp. Will
you be like this hunter if your time comes to
spend an unplanned night or two in the woods?

How to Use This Little Book

1. When you first get this book, sit down and **READ it**. Think about what you are reading and how it can apply to you and your outings.

2. Reread the chapter entitled **"Survival Kit"** and make a list of the items you need to purchase to put one together.

3. On a weekend you want to do something that is fun and educational, take your survival kit into the woods and spend the night using the items in the kit. Upon completion of the **overnight test**, be sure to replace any items that may be difficult to repack into a compact package. This exercise may also help you discover items you will want in your survival kit that my list did not include. Remember it is YOUR survival kit, so modify it to meet your needs.

4. **This book does not go into navigational skills.** I feel this requires training that, like first aid, you should have before you start exploring the backcountry. If you haven't had training in the proper use of your GPS or map and compass, get it ASAP. That alone can keep you from ever needing this book.

5. **This book covers only the most basic first-aid skills.** It is my belief that everyone who ventures into the backcountry should have successfully taken a Red Cross first-aid course. Also, those who have special medical conditions should be skilled in managing them.

6. **Place this book in your survival kit** so it will be there if, and when, you need it to guide you through a survival situation. It was designed to be small enough to fit into your kit, and concise enough to be a quick and easy resource when you are in trouble.

7. Be sure you always read, then practice the information found in the chapter entitled **"Before You Go."** This will help keep your time in a survival situation short.

8. If you find yourself in a lost or stranded situation, **stop, sit down, think, remain calm, don't panic and plan to stay put.** By gaining control of yourself in these first few minutes, you have increased your chances of survival by 50 percent.

9. When you first realize you are lost and in trouble is the time to dig this book out and use it to guide you toward a safe wait until you are found.

10. As a Maine game warden once said, "Even in today's modern world there are many trappers and guides that spend the night in the woods with little more than what is found in a basic survival kit, they spend their lives doing it. Relax—you may even enjoy your unplanned stay in the woods."

Take a first-aid course and keep your training up to date. You may have to treat your own injuries in a survival emergency.

Modern Search & Rescue Works for You

If you have taken the time and precaution to file a trip plan with a responsible person before your outing, then should you not return on time, you will not go unnoticed for very long. This will begin a series of events that will result in your being rescued quickly.

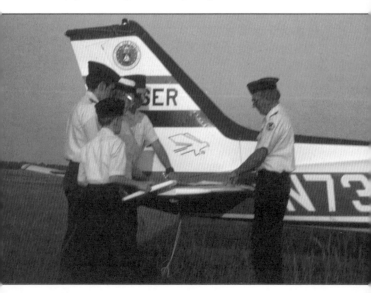

One of the most common, and dangerous, fears most lost or stranded people have is that no one will know to come looking for them. If you have followed the steps in the next chapter of this book, then you can put this fear to rest; trained people will be looking for you soon. If you stay put once you realize you are lost, then it will take even less time to find you. Trying to walk out, panicking and running will work against you; and it will take much longer for rescuers to find you. For every hour a lost person walks, the search area grows four times larger. You should stay put and wait to be found!

Here Is How It Works

A search starts quickly when you are reported missing to local authorities. In most cases, this is the county sheriff, district forest ranger or conservation officer. In Canada it is usually the Royal Canadian Mounted Police. Today, many of these officers have received formal training in search and rescue organization and know how to respond quickly to a missing outdoorsman emergency.

Many missing people give up hope quickly because they think no one is looking for them. Modern search and rescue is usually on the site within a few hours.

When a missing outdoorsman report is turned in, the first thing that usually happens is a "search boss" is designated. This is someone with a lot of experience and training in back-country searches. He organizes the search and establishes priorities. He will ensure that the site where the person was last seen is quickly protected, set up a search headquarters and interview those people who were last with the missing person.

Protecting the "last seen" area keeps well-meaning people from destroying tracks and other important signs expert trackers will need for tracking the lost person.

The interview with the missing person's friends/family is most important, as this is

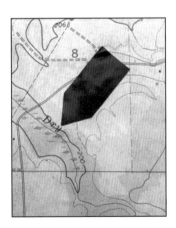

where the search boss learns much about the missing person. If a trip plan has been left with someone, it will cut down on the time it takes to get an

The search director will quickly establish the "area of probability" and the search will be centered there.

Early in the search, specially trained dogs may be used
to trail the missing person. Two to four aircraft are used
to quickly locate missing outdoorsmen.

organized search started. They will have a good
idea where to begin looking.

The interviewer will be looking for detailed
information on the missing person. The person's
name, address, description, clothing worn, boot
type (sole information is important to trackers),

age, equipment he has with him, medical conditions including medications, experience in the outdoors, physical condition, personality traits, etc. All of this information is important to experienced searchers because it tells them a lot about where to look for the missing person.

Usually the first searchers to hit the trail include trackers with dogs and a hasty team. The hasty team is made up of highly specialized people who go into the most likely areas the missing person is believed to be. This is why it is important to stay put when you first realize you are lost.

At the same time, lookouts and road check teams are posted. Lookouts are located at observation points in the search area and road search teams ride roads near the search area looking for the missing person.

As quickly as possible, aircraft will be brought into the search; often aircraft with specialized equipment to electronically help find the missing person. At that point, the search boss may set up grid searches supervised by professionals and carried out using volunteers.

Many people who are lost fear searchers will only look a few hours then give up, thinking the missing person is dead. This is not true. Most search bosses estimate how long the missing person can survive under the conditions and then plan to search three times that long, if needed. Search efforts go far beyond reasonable expectations.

Lost and stranded people should never give up hope. The search will go on until you are rescued. How fast that search begins, however, depends upon how well you prepared before you went into the woods!

Aircraft are used to quickly locate missing outdoorsmen.

2. BEFORE YOU GO

A quick rescue actually begins before you get lost or stranded. It begins with you taking

File a trip plan with a responsible person. Let him know exactly where you are going and when you plan on returning.

some precautions before you leave home, camp or your vehicle. Here is a checklist of precautions:

1. Study maps and get to know the territory you will be going into. Take the map and navigational equipment that you know how to use with you. USE IT FROM THE BEGINNING OF YOUR OUTING.

2. Learn the area's weather extremes. Know what to expect in sudden weather changes. Dress for it.

3. Listen to an NOAA weather report for the period you expect to be in the area.

4. Carry a freshly charged cell phone and/or a two-way radio with fresh batteries.

5. Pack a survival kit.

6. Carry a knife on your belt.

7. MOST IMPORTANT: FILE A TRIP PLAN WITH A RESPONSIBLE PERSON!!!!

Always use a GPS and/or map and compass on all outings. Make this a practice and chances are good you will never need to use survival skills.

Sample Trip Plan

- ☐ Name:
- ☐ Address:
- ☐ Emergency phone number:
- ☐ Coordinates of destination:
- ☐ Further description of destination:
- ☐ Purpose of trip:
- ☐ Mode of transportation:
- ☐ Departure date and time:
- ☐ Return date and time:
- ☐ Name of others with you:

If you are departing from a vehicle, be sure to park the vehicle in an area where it can be found easily. Leave a slip of paper in a clear plastic bag with your name, emergency phone number, date and time of departure, description of destination and expected return date and time. Place this bag under the windshield wiper of the vehicle. This will probably be the starting point of the search when the person you left your trip plan with notifies the authorities you are missing. Also, this serves as a backup in case something happens to the person you left responsible to monitor your trip plan.

Taking these precautions are as important as packing a survival kit. If a responsible person doesn't know you are overdue from your scheduled return, regardless of how short the trip, then no one will know to start looking for you. People have been lost for days before anyone realized there was a problem. In these cases survival ceased to be a short-term emergency and became a long-term nightmare, often with a disastrous ending.

DON'T FAIL TO TAKE THESE PRECAUTIONS!

Assemble Your Own Survival Kit

The individual survival kit weighs only two pounds and contains the items necessary to survive an unplanned night in the woods. It will keep you safe if you know how to use it and take it with you.

Go on outdoor adventures prepared to spend three extra, unexpected days in the backcountry. To do this, you need to take with you items that will:

1. Provide quick protection from inclement weather.

2. Retain body heat.

3. Help start a fire.

4. Provide safe drinking water.

5. Offer protection from biting insects.

6. Provide two methods of signaling for help beyond a cell phone or two-way radio.

These items make up your personal survival kit. When combined with your belt knife or multi-tool, map, compass and GPS, they give you the edge you'll need to survive.

The survival kit is important not only for its lifesaving merits, but for comfort on those outings when a night must be spent unexpectedly in the woods or streamside. I have been forced on many occasions to spend a night or two in the woods I didn't plan on, because an outfitter was late picking me up, climbing down a mountain in the dark was too dangerous, a motor conked out on my boat, etc. Each time, my two-pound survival kit provided me with a comfortable camp. Without it the wait would have been cold and dangerous.

Suggested Items for the Personal Survival Kit

- ☐ Tube tent
- ☐ Strike-anywhere kitchen matches in waterproof match safe
- ☐ Flashlight
- ☐ Fire starters
- ☐ Signal mirror
- ☐ Police whistle
- ☐ MPI Emergency Space bag
- ☐ Parachute cord – 50'
- ☐ Aluminum foil – 36" x 36"
- ☐ Insect repellent
- ☐ Water purification tablets
- ☐ Pocket Survival Guide
- ☐ First Aid Kit

SHELTER — The first item necessary for a survival camp is shelter. You can read all you want about a lean-to, brush shelters, etc., but few shelters are quicker to erect and give as much protection as a plastic tube tent. You simply tie a strong cord between two trees, stretch the tube to its full 8-foot length and crawl in out of the weather. I use the Coghlan's Tube Tent. It is compact, weighs 18 ounces and is a bright orange color, serving as a signal that can be easily seen from the air. Not only have I used a tube tent in a survival situation, I have used one on several occasions for protection from a sudden rain or hail storm when I didn't have a rain suit or other protection.

SLEEP WARM — To stay warm in your tube tent, you will want one of the 36" x 84" MPI Emergency Space bags. This bag, which folds up to 1½" x 3" and weighs only 4 ounces, will reflect and retain 90 percent of radiated body heat. You will need to be careful using one of these bags when you are wearing boots with aggressive soles as they can cause the blanket to tear. But, with a little caution when getting into the bag, it will keep you warm all night. When on guided hunts I carry an extra bag; I want my guide to be rested in order to get me out safely the next day. Also, an extra bag, while weighing little and taking up little space in my survival kit, gives me a backup if I should tear the first one.

MATCHES — To build a fire you will need fresh strike-anywhere kitchen matches in a waterproof match safe. I use the full-size wooden matches because they are easy to ignite and burn longer than small book or box matches. I keep them in a weathertight safety orange plastic match safe. Replace them often as matches have a short shelf life.

FIRE STARTERS — Since starting a fire can be difficult, especially in windy or damp conditions, a package of fire starters is a must. Campmor's has a 4-ounce package of 20 Fire Lighters, each of which burn seven minutes. These can be used for boiling water as easily as starting a campfire.

SIGNAL MIRROR — Two methods of signaling, beyond a cell phone or two-way radio, should be carried. I suggest a signal mirror, such as Star Flash, and a high-quality whistle, such as a Fox 40 whistle. The signal mirror is easy to use and can be seen more than 60 miles away.

WHISTLE — The whistle requires very little energy to use, can be heard much farther than the human voice and lasts much longer. Get a whistle that has a contrasting color, such as yellow or bright orange, and a lanyard so that it may be worn around the neck for fast use when in a survival situation.

INSECT REPELLENT — For protection against mosquitoes, ticks, chiggers and other biting insects, I carry a small packet of insect repellent. During warm weather it is worth its weight in gold, especially at night when mosquitoes are flying.

FLASHLIGHT — I include a small flashlight in my kit. I like the ones that use lithium batteries due to their 10-year shelf life. The flashlight can be used for signaling and is a must for doing camp chores in the dark. Select a quality compact flashlight such as the Streamlight Twin-Task or Sure-Fire E2 Executive.

ALUMINUM FOIL — One of the most versatile items I carry in my survival kit is a 36" x 36" piece of heavy-duty aluminum foil folded up to about 3" x 3". It can be used to make a vessel for boiling water or cooking food, to make a reflector for a fire and as a signal mirror.

WATER PURIFICATION TABLETS — While food need not be a concern for the 72-hour survival ordeal, water will be necessary. Since safe drinking water has become scarce even in the most remote wilderness areas, it is a good idea to take along a small bottle of Potable Aqua tablets to treat drinking water. Be sure to follow instructions carefully.

GALLON-SIZE RESEALABLE PLASTIC BAG — Pack your survival kit in a one-gallon resealable bag, such as Ziplock. It can be used to hold water while treating with water purification tablets.

PARACHUTE CORD — Carry a 50-foot length of parachute cord. You will find it serves many purposes, especially when improvising a shelter. If small, strong string is needed, the parachute cord can be cut open and the many small strings, which make up the core of the cord, can be used separately to repair clothing, close an end of the tube tent, etc.

POCKET SURVIVAL GUIDE — Don't forget to place a copy of this book in the kit. It can be an invaluable resource to refer to when caught in an unexpected situation. This survival kit will fit into a coat pocket or daypack and cost from $40 to $100, depending upon the cost of the flashlight. It is not sufficient to purchase all these items and put them in your daypack, tackle box or hunting coat pocket to be there when you need them. Like any specialized outdoor gear, you need to give them a field test. Actually use them overnight, so you are familiar with them when you need them most.

OTHER IMPORTANT ITEMS — If you require special medications, such as injections to counteract stinging insects, then by all means include this in your gear. Some people include a Power Bar in their survival kit. I always carry bottled water in my daypack on outings. Don't load yourself down with unnecessary items, but include those which you deem necessary for your safety.

When you use items from your survival kit, make it a high priority to replace them ASAP.

SOURCES OF SURVIVAL KIT ITEMS — Most survival items mentioned can be found in good camping supply stores or by going to the following Web sites:

www.campmor.com
www.foxridgeoutfitters.com
www.epcamps.com
www.cabelas.com
www.mpioutdoors.com

POCKET FIRST-AID KIT
- Sterile dressing

- Gauze roller bandage or elastic roller bandage (Ace Wrap)

- Adhesive bandages (Band-Aids™)

- Wound closure strips (heavy-duty butterfly adhesive bandages)

- Adhesive or duct tape

- Polysporin or Double Antibiotic Ointment

- Tweezers and safety pins

BASIC SURVIVAL FIRST AID

The following recommendations are based on the assumption that the survivor is alone and will have to treat himself.

BLEEDING

You must control serious bleeding immediately!

Arterial Bleeding — Arteries carry blood away from the heart. Blood from a cut artery appears bright red and comes in distinct spurts that match the rhythm of the heartbeat. Arterial blood is under high pressure and a cut artery can result in the loss of a large volume of blood in a short period of time. Arterial bleeding must be controlled immediately or death may result.

Venous Bleeding — Veins carry blood back to the heart. Blood from a severed vein will appear dark red or bluish in color and will come in a steady flow. Venous bleeding is more easily controlled than arterial bleeding.

Capillary Bleeding — Bleeding from capillaries, small vessels that connect arteries and veins, commonly occurs as a result of small cuts and abrasions. Capillary bleeding is easily controlled.

Direct Pressure — The most effective way to control external bleeding is direct pressure applied over the wound. The pressure must be firm enough to stop the blood flow and should be maintained long enough to close the damaged surface. Whenever possible, the bleeding part should be elevated above the level of the heart—for example, by raising a limb.

Pressure Dressing — If bleeding continues after pressure has been applied for about 30 minutes, you should apply a pressure dressing. This should be a thick dressing of gauze or other material applied directly over the wound and held in place by a tightly wrapped bandage. The bandage should not be so tight as to restrict circulation. Keep the dressing in place.

Tourniquet — Use a tourniquet only in cases of massive wounds with severe bleeding or when direct pressure cannot control bleeding. A tourniquet should only be placed on the upper leg or arms. Place a tourniquet between the wound and the heart, never directly over the injury or fracture. Use a stick to tighten the tourniquet just enough to stop the flow of blood. Bind the free end of the stick to the limb. Cut-off blood flow can result in the loss of a limb. A lone survivor should not release the tourniquet. Under normal circumstances a tourniquet should be loosened every 10 to 15 minutes to restore blood flow to the limb but this can be risky if you are by yourself.

WOUNDS

In most survival situations it is best not to try to close a wound. Leave the wound open to allow drainage from any infection that may occur. Cover the wound with a clean dressing and bandage and change the dressing daily if possible. In the case of a gaping wound, you can close the edges with a "butterfly" adhesive strip made from adhesive tape or a Band-Aid™.

SPRAINS

Sprains are the stretching or tearing of ligaments when a joint is twisted beyond its normal range of motion. Ice or some form of cold should be applied, if possible, to the injured area to reduce swelling. Heat should not be used since it will encourage internal capillary bleeding and increase swelling. A compression wrap, made by placing some form of padding over the injured joint and wrapping with an elastic bandage, will prevent swelling and give support. Where possible the injured joint should be elevated above the level of the heart to reduce swelling.

FRACTURES

Relocating or setting bones will be difficult for a lone survivor. A simple fracture can be treated by immobilizing the injured limb with an improvised splint to reduce pain and prevent further injury.

The above procedures are recommended in the U.S. ARMY SURVIVAL MANUAL FM 21-76.

4. WEATHER

Equip Yourself for Local Weather Conditions

Bad weather is often the cause of people getting stranded in the outdoors. One of the most valuable tools any outdoorsman can have in his base camp, vehicle or while on an outing is a small NOAA (National Oceanic and Atmospheric Administration) weather-band radio. They can be purchased at many outdoor stores and electronic stores such as Radio Shack. The NOAA Weather Radio System broadcasts timely weather information for local areas across the United States on a 24-hour-a-day basis. The network is capable of reaching 90 percent of all Americans. Canada has a similar system called Weatheradio Canada.

Some weather-band radios are equipped with an alarm feature so that they will automatically turn on when severe weather threatens. Most of the weather-band radios operate on a battery, making them convenient to carry into the backcountry. Make a weather-band radio a must-have item of equipment for your base camp or vehicle. Use it prior to every outing! Before going into the woods for any period of time, take a few minutes and listen to the weather-band radio for forecasts of the weather during the period you will be outside. Then, dress for the weather.

Before going afield, listen to a current weather report and dress for the worst of the expected weather. Expect the unexpected.

DRESS FOR THE UNEXPECTED — Even in areas of mild weather the temperature can change dramatically as the time of day changes. Deserts that are hot during the day can be cold at night. Sudden rain showers can change a mild day into a cold one. Climbing steep mountains can cause a person to sweat, making his clothing wet, which can then make him feel cold in the wind.

The point is, always expect the unexpected when planning an outing. It does not take much space in a daypack to include a lightweight rain suit. It may even come in handy on a dry day as a windbreaker. If you get lost or stranded, you could be out a day or two longer than expected. During that time, the weather could dramatically change.

Dress for the expected weather temperature extremes for the period you intend to be out. Dress in layers so that you can remove clothing and put in your daypack as the temperature warms up or you exert yourself. As the temperature drops, or you slow your pace, you can put the layers back on.

Most importantly, don't go off without a hat. During cool or cold weather, as much as 75 percent of your body heat loss can be through the uncovered head. This can be critical during a period of survival, especially during the night when you are trying to rest.

Wear clothing to match the climate and listen to the weather-band radio for changes. Don't push your luck in bad weather. A day spent in camp during dense fog, snowstorm, thunderstorms, etc., is much better than a night in a survival camp wishing you had canceled the outing.

You Are in Trouble — Stop!

Your most important survival skill is your ability to admit that you are lost or stranded. That is not an easy decision to make. Most people will not admit that until they have wandered around for long periods getting into a worse situation than they would have been in had they recognized their predicament at the beginning.

Once you admit that you are lost or stranded, sit down and think. If you have a cell phone or two-way radio, now is the time to call for help and await the help. Get control of yourself, avoid panic and stay calm. Mentally, you must accept the challenge you are facing and make the best of the adventure. If you left a trip plan with a responsible person before you left, chances are that people will be looking for you soon. Your adventure will be short lived. Even in remote regions of North America, 99 percent of the missing people on outings are found within 72 hours or less. You will be too.

Let's face it, avoiding panic is difficult when dealing with yourself or, if you are not alone, with those people around you when fear begins to set in. Most people who get lost or stranded panic to some degree but those who fare best get control of their thoughts quickly. In extreme

When you first realize you are lost or stranded, STOP then and relax. Your mind is your best survival tool if it is calm and thinking rationally.

cases, those who panic may forget who they are or where they are. Some even hide from searchers. This erratic behavior makes it difficult for searchers to find them. Here is a good way to manage panic:

STOP

The first thing to do when you admit to yourself that you are lost or stranded is to resist the temptation to walk or run your way out of the situation. STOP! This is the acronym for:

Sit
Think
Observe
Plan

Follow this simple plan of controlling panic.

Sit — The act of sitting down will help keep you from getting into deeper trouble. This one act alone can also jump-start the thinking process, and it helps suppress the urge to run or to make hasty, foolish decisions. You will need this time to get over the shock that it has happened to you: YOU ARE LOST.

Think — Survival is the challenge to stay alive. Your mind is the best survival tool you have. In such a situation, you are at the mercy of your mind. In order to survive, you must keep in control by thinking of past training, by maintaining a positive mental attitude and by developing the determination to survive.

Think about your priorities. The priorities of survival are known as the Rules of Three:

1. You may be doomed in three seconds if you let panic rule.

2. You cannot live more than three minutes without oxygen.

3. You cannot live more than three hours in temperature extremes without body shelter.

4. You cannot live more than three days without water.

5. You will need food in three weeks.

These priorities tell you that you need to think of the real and immediate dangers, not those conjured up by your fears. Your most immediate danger is your own mind. Don't let fear take control and cloud clear, resourceful thinking.

Observe — Observe your surroundings to discover what problems must be solved and what resources you have to solve them. You will need shelter, signals, fire, water and a campsite that is easily spotted. Select a campsite, get out your survival kit and set about getting ready to be found. If you are with others, make job assignments. Get everyone involved. Keep everyone busy. Keep everyone positive.

Plan — Now that you are settled down and ready to live the adventure, make plans to set them in motion.

1. Select a survival campsite near an open area or your stalled vehicle.

2. Set up a set of signals, with backups, and keep them ready for instant use.

3. Erect your tube tent or construct shelter making it reasonably comfortable without wasting energy.

4. Gather firewood and start a fire.

5. Maintain a positive survival spirit.

6. Dispel fears.

7. Boost the will to live.

8. Get comfortable, enjoy the unique experience and get ready to be found. It will not take long.

6. SIGNALS

Prepare Your Signals

Waving bright clothing or other gear in an open area can get the attention of a search aircraft.

Whether you are lost or stranded, the first step to being found is to leave a trip plan with a responsi-

You need to be able to hear the searchers, so try to avoid a survival campsite near noisy waters.

ble person. Next, you need to be seen or heard. Assuming you have let someone know where you are going and when you expect to return, it won't be long before someone will be looking for you in the area in which you are located. Your first concern should be to prepare to be seen, or heard, by the rescue party.

Try to avoid making your survival camp near a waterfall or roaring creek. You need to be where you can hear searchers and a survival camp in these locations drown out sounds made by searchers and sometimes your signals to them.

Signaling is a survival skill that no one should take lightly, especially since we now have excellent search aircraft that can be in the air over the search area soon after a person is reported missing. Also, hasty teams of experienced searchers can be on the ground looking for a missing person within a few hours after he or she is reported missing.

Here are some of the best signaling methods, second only to a working two-way radio or cell phone:

SIGNAL MIRROR — Most survival experts consider the signal mirror to be one of the best signal devices available. They are small and easy to carry in a survival kit, coat or daypack. It amazes people how far a reflection from these little mirrors can be seen.

United States Air Force rescue planes have spotted a signal mirror from as far away as 100 miles. Distances of 30 to 40 miles are common. Several times lost people have used a signal mirror to attract the attention of rangers in a forest fire tower or searchers miles away on a mountainside or in a flat desert.

A Texas pilot was flying home from Alaska when his helicopter crashed in a thick spruce forest in British Columbia. For 14 days he sur-

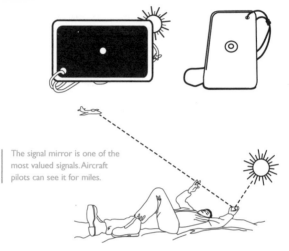

The signal mirror is one of the most valued signals. Aircraft pilots can see it for miles.

vived at the crash site. He was found due to using a piece of shiny metal as a signal mirror to get the attention of a search and rescue plane as it flew over. Many downed combat pilots and military special ops units in Southeast Asia during the 1960s and 70s owe their lives to a signal mirror.

Signal mirrors may be purchased at many out-door supply stores and there are numerous sources found when you search the Web. Today, most signal mirrors are made from tough plastic and have instructions on the back. While the instructions are easy to follow, no one should wait until they get in a survival situation before

The signal mirror is quick and easy to use. Practice the aiming and correct use of the signal mirror at home before going afield.

they learn how to use it properly. Practice until you understand the proper way to use the mirror.

Most signal mirrors have a hole in the center for aiming. They are used to reflect the sun, moon or aircraft searchlight to signal an over-head aircraft, boat or other target such as a search party that is within view but a long distance away. Here is how to use the signal mirror:

1. Hold the mirror in front of your eye so you can see through the hole.

2. Make sure the shiny side is toward the sun, moon or searchlight.

3. Take your other hand and hold it out at arm's length.

4. Reflect light onto the extended hand.

5. While looking through the aiming hole, turn the mirror in order to swing the reflected spot toward the target.

6. Keep your signal mirror with you and be prepared to use it fast.

Signal mirrors may be improvised from almost any shiny object, such as aluminum foil, a car mirror, the bottom out of a tin can with a hole in the center or even a CD. In fact, a CD makes an excellent signal mirror, due to its highly reflective surface and the hole in the center that can be used as an aiming device.

POLICE WHISTLE — A loud whistle such as those used by police, coaches and dog handlers makes an excellent signal device. It is easy to carry, requires little energy to use, can be heard much farther than the human voice and lasts long after a shouting person becomes hoarse. The whistle makes a good signal when a ground party is conducting the search. The whistle is easily heard and if tracking dogs are being used, they can hear it from great distances.

To use a whistle effectively, stay calm and do not blow the whistle until it is thought that someone is within hearing distance. To blow a whistle continuously for hours when no one is around only wastes vital energy and brings on frustration. When you think enough time has gone by and people are likely looking for you, try giving a few blows on your whistle every 30 minutes just in case someone is out there, and then whistle them in. When you hear searchers, stay put and let them come to you.

FIRE — One of the best-known signals, both day and night, is a fire. At night, a bright campfire in an opening can be seen for miles from the air and a fair distance on the ground, especially in mountains. During the day, the same fire can be made to smoke when wet leaves or green vegetation is piled on it. Smoke during the day is an excellent signal.

Remember to be extremely careful when making and using a signal fire.

The survival campfire can be a good day or night signal if properly used.

When in a survival situation, most people are upset and excited and mistakes come easily. You are in enough trouble already without getting caught in a forest fire that you have set.

Carry kitchen matches in a waterproof container and a fire starter with you. Know how to start a fire even in wet conditions. Building a fire in a survival situation is more difficult than most people think. Master the skill of fire making before you actually need it.

FLASHLIGHT — One of the new generations of ultra bright flashlights, such as those by SureFire or Streamlight, makes an excellent signal at night. If the flashlight has an on-off switch that allows you to signal "SOS" in Morse code, so much the better. Three short flashes, three long flashes, and three short flashes are the "SOS" signal known to all rescue personnel. Even a small light out in the open can be seen a long way by aircraft at night.

BRIGHT CLOTHING & EQUIPMENT — The bright orange clothing many hunters wear works well as a signal, especially if aircraft is used in a search. Even a white T-shirt or yellow rain suit can be used as a signal panel. Brightly colored equipment such as a red tube tent or orange pack has been used to signal searchers. The bottom line is to find something that stands out from the terrain you are in.

GROUND-TO-AIR SIGNALS — Search pilots are all familiar with ground-to-air signals. These are large symbols the lost or stranded person forms out in the OPEN where they can be seen by search aircraft. They must contrast with the ground to be seen. Dark limbs on snow or light colored rocks on dark soil are examples of what has proven useful.

The signal must be large to be seen from the air. For example the "X," the universal signal for help, should have legs that are 3 feet in width and a single leg length of 18 feet.

Ground-to-air signals should have lines that are 3 feet wide and 18 feet long to be seen by search aircraft.

Ground-to-Air Signals

Here are the symbols search pilots recognize. Remember the "X" is the one used most often:

 1. Require doctor – serious injuries

2. Require medical supplies

 3. Unable to proceed

4. Require food and water

5. Require firearms and ammunition

 6. Indicate direction to proceed

 7. Am proceeding in this direction

8. Will attempt to take off

9. Aircraft badly damaged

 10. Probably safe to land here

 11. All well

12. Require fuel and oil

13. No – negative

14. Yes – affirmative

 15. Not understood

16. Require engineer

17. Require compass and map

 18. Require signal lamp

GUNSHOTS — Gunshots can be a good signal, and they carry a long distance; however, they must be used at the right time to be effective. If you are in trouble during hunting season your shots may be mistaken as shots from hunters. Save your ammunition and wait until well after dark. Then fire three shots into the air. Listen for three shots in return. If you make contact, fire only one shot when you hear your searchers shoot. Save your ammo as it may take several shots to guide them in. If you get no response, save your ammo and don't shoot again until you hear sounds from your searchers. If there is no one near enough to hear your gunshots or if they are confused with hunters, it will only be a waste of ammo and bring no help.

It is important to know how to use signals properly, and that you have the signals ready for use on short notice. Also, it is important to choose an open area to do your signaling. Many signals will not be seen from the air if you sit under a thick canopy of tall trees to await rescue. Select an open area, if possible, to wait for your rescuers and have your signals ready. Areas, such as old roads, fields, sites of old forest fires, sea- or lakeshore or any other type of opening will help you be seen early in the search. Remember to stay where you are, and don't give in to the urge to travel. Signaling will bring help to you.

Construct
a Shelter

Shelter is often the first priority of survival. In this case, shelter from 120-degree heat is sought by digging into the ground under a disabled truck. The truck became an oven in this heat.

Shelter is defined as a "place affording protection from the elements." Every survivor, faced with the problem of protecting himself from the elements, must consider using every conceivable place already existing in his immediate area or using every available material at hand to improvise a place that will afford much-needed protection. When deciding what type of shelter to build, you must first consider what the shelter is to protect you from, i.e., rain, cold, insects, heat. As an example, when in hot, arid areas, protection from the sun during the day may be the prime consideration. In frigid areas, extreme cold aggravated by high winds or, in some seasons, swarms of insects may be the dangers that dictate what type of protection the survivor must seek.

In addition to protection from natural elements and conditions, an adequate shelter also provides the survivor with psychological well-being, so necessary for sound rest. Adequate rest is extremely important if the survivor is to make sound decisions. The need for rest becomes more critical as time passes and rescue is prolonged. Rest contributes to mental and physical health, and adequate shelter contributes to sound rest. Because of these factors, adequate shelter must be placed high on the priority list if survival is to be successful.

Constructing shelter for your survival camp may or may not be a rush matter. If the weather is mild with no rain, you may postpone constructing a shelter. However, if the weather is bad or subject to get worse, then shelter construction may become very high on your list of priorities. One plus for shelter construction, assuming you are in good shape, is that it keeps you occupied. Constructing a good shelter where you can rest comfortably out of the elements takes time and some work, but this will help keep your mind off your troubles.

The location of your shelter site will depend on several things. The first priority is that it be in a location where search aircraft or ground parties can easily see you. I was once leading a ground search party looking for two lost hikers. It took us two days longer than it should have to find the hikers due to the hidden location they had selected to set up their survival camp.

If you are stranded with a vehicle, plane, boat, snowmobile or canoe, try to either use the craft as a camp or set up your shelter nearby due to their high visibility. The exception to this would be if the craft were hidden by thick brush or trees.

If you are walking or skiing, select an open area, if possible, in which to set up your survival camp. This may require that you cut some brush or small trees. Avoid constructing your shelter in a low swamp area or in a dry creek bed. Your predicament is bad enough without getting caught in a flash flood or rising ground water. Also, in warm weather, mosquitoes may be a problem.

Look up before selecting a shelter site. Don't build your shelter under standing dead trees or dead limbs or branches heavy with snow. These could fall on you. Avoid thick overhead vegetation that could block the view for aircraft as well as conceal your distress signals. Avoid avalanche-prone slopes. Try to construct your shelter so that you can sleep comfortably. Select a level or near level site. Remove stones and sticks. Your sleep is vital to conserve energy for survival.

Set up a ground-to-air signal as soon as you have a survival campsite selected. If the weather is not too bad, set your signals up before you construct your shelter. Waiting may cause you to miss a chance for early rescue.

If possible, find an opening and set up your shelter near a source of water such as a spring, creek, river or lake. Not only does this save energy in getting water, but it also is a good place to find animals and plants for food. Other people visit areas near water more frequently, thus increasing your chances of being discovered.

The type of shelter you select to use in your survival camp will be based on several factors:

1. What shelter material do you have with you — tube tent, vehicle, canoe, airplane, tarp, emergency blanket, sheet of plastic, etc?

2. What equipment do you have to aid in shelter construction — axe, saw, knife, rope, etc?

3. What natural materials are available for shelter construction — rocks, trees, poles, snow, cave, etc?

4. What is the weather like now? What kind of weather do you expect?

5. What is the season of the year?

How effective your shelter will be will depend upon what you have to construct it with and what the weather is like, plus your ability to improvise and any previous training you have had in shelter construction.

Tube Tent

If you are traveling in the backcountry by foot, ATV, vehicle, plane, snowmobile, canoe, boat, horseback or skis, you would be smart to take a tent with you. I learned while working in northern Canada and Alaska to have a tube tent with me at all times. I have spent many unplanned nights in the wilderness. The tube tent is easy and quick to set up. You simply run a rope or cords through the plastic tube and tie it between two trees. Since they blow like a sail in high wind, it is a good idea to weigh down the front and rear openings with rocks or heavy logs.

The tube tent you pack in your survival kit is one of the best quick shelters available.

A lean-to made from a Space blanket or tarp is an effective shelter and is simple to erect.

Lean-to

A tarp, or an emergency blanket, especially one in a bright orange color, makes an extremely versatile shelter. It can be stretched over an open boat to make a cozy shelter. It can be stretched alongside an overturned canoe to form a lean-to. You can also stretch it from a wing of a plane to the ground or from the side of a vehicle to the ground. It makes a good lean-to, especially when trying to escape desert heat. A rainproof lean-to is good in cold weather because when used with a reflector fire, the shelter can be comfortable in the worst of weather.

Space Blanket

The MPI Space blanket, which is sold in many camping supply stores, is a good item to carry in a personal survival kit. This blanket is made from a very thin but strong space-age material that can reflect 90 percent of the heat thrown against it. It is compact, about the size of a pack of cigarettes. It can be made into a lean-to, and when used with a reflector fire, is very warm. This blanket makes a warm sleeping bag when folded properly.

Any type of plastic that is large enough can be made into a lean-to. This includes cutting plastic garbage bags so that they make a square sheet.

Natural Shelters

A rock overhang or cave makes one of the best natural shelters to be found. In fact, during the 1700s, the longhunters who were exploring the wilderness west of the Appalachian Mountains spent entire winters in survival-type camps they made under rock overhangs. By building up rock or log walls as windbreaks, these shelters can actually be comfortable. One downside, though, due to their locations: They are usually difficult to spot from the air or from any great distance on the ground, making rescue much more difficult. Locating ground-to-air signals nearby is a must when using these types of shelters.

Many times, freshly blown-down trees can be made into a survival shelter by cutting away the limbs near the ground. If large pieces of bark are around, use them to improve the roof.

A natural shelter, such as this rock overhang, may be found in the survival area. Due to it being somewhat hidden from the air, ground-to-air signals should be set up.

Snow Shelters

In the winter there are several survival shelters that can be constructed. However, shelters such as the famous snow cave take a lot of energy and skill. The hole-in-the-snow shelter is one of the simpler shelters if the snow is at least 4 feet deep.

Hole-in-the-Snow Shelter — Find an evergreen tree that has limbs extending down to snow level, then dig out all the snow around its trunk right down to the ground. Next, trim all the inside branches and use them to line the bottom and finish the top. Since this shelter is hidden, be sure to keep your ground-to-air signals out and clean of snow.

Snow Cave — A snow cave is an excellent cold weather shelter, but it requires a lot of energy, a shovel or similar device, and some skill. Begin by finding a packed snowdrift that is about 7 feet high and 12 feet or more wide. Then start digging a low tunnel into the snowbank. After you dig the tunnel 2 feet into the snowbank, hollow out an opening large enough for you to lie down.

Next, push a stick through the roof at a 45-degree angle to make a vent hole. In the back of the cave, build the bed platform at least 18

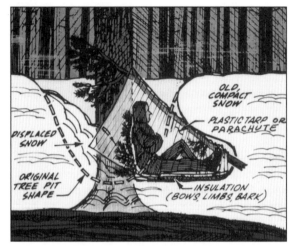

OLD, COMPACT SNOW

PLASTIC TARP OR PARACHUTE

DISPLACED SNOW

ORIGINAL TREE PIT SHAPE

INSULATION (BOWS, LIMBS, BARK)

A hole-in-the-snow shelter can be dug in snow-covered areas by digging a pit at the base of evergreen trees with low-hanging branches.

inches high. To conserve heat, the cave should be built just large enough to sleep, dress and undress while lying in the sleeping bag. If desired, the sleeping shelf may be walled in to conserve heat. In addition to the ventilation hole through the roof, there should be another at the door if you push snow into the opening to block the outside elements.

Since they cannot be heated many degrees above freezing, life in snow shelters is rugged. It takes several weeks to acclimate yourself to the effects of living in such a cold atmosphere. You will require more food and hot drinks.

Regardless of how cold it may get outside, the temperature inside a small, well-constructed snow cave probably will not be lower than -10°F, and with a candle, it can be heated to 32°F. Snow caves are difficult for searchers to find. Good signals are a must.

There are many other crude shelters that can be made. The secret to shelter construction is simple—use what is available to protect yourself from the elements. Construct whatever shelter uses the least amount of energy to build and, if possible, set it up where it can be seen. In most cases, the tube tent you carry in your survival kit will be the best emergency shelter.

Constructed in a snowdrift or bank, a snow cave shelter makes effective use of the insulating qualities of snow. The wall should be at least 17 inches thick.

Build a Survival Fire

Fire serves many valuable purposes in the survival camp. Can you build a fire on a cold, wet, windy day with just one match?

You realize you are lost or, perhaps, stranded. You have stopped and calmed down. You have wisely decided to wait for rescue. Finding a nearby opening in the woods where your signals can be seen from the air, you take out your survival kit and locate your waterproof match container and fire starter and build a fire. Sounds easy, doesn't it? But, what if you didn't have matches? What if you didn't know how to build a fire? The unknowing might say you can always start a fire with flint and steel or with a fire drill or with a lens from your glasses. The unknowing might also say anybody can build a fire. How wrong this kind of thinking can be.

First, let's establish how valuable a fire can be to a lost or stranded person. Most people lost in the backcountry are scared, embarrassed, lonely, hungry, often cold or being attacked by flying pests, bored and usually in poor spirits. A fire can solve many of these problems. A survival fire serves as a signal, keeps the lost person busy, drives away pests, provides warmth, purifies water, dries clothing, lifts spirits, cooks food, gives light and may be used in crafting many useful items. Fire gives a sense of security and, in a way, provides company. Flame can harden a wooden spear point. The white ashes can be consumed to overcome constipation, the black ashes to stop diarrhea. In short, fire is one of the most valuable aids to your survival.

Use your knife to get into the dry wood found in the center of a damp log.

Except for a handful of experts, there are few among us who can start a fire without matches or a lighter. Flint and steel, fire drill, fire plow, etc., make interesting demonstrations but seldom work in a real survival camp. Also, they use a lot of energy. Despite what many survival books say, there are few substitutes for fresh, dry wooden strike-anywhere kitchen matches and prepackaged fire starters (such as Coghlan's Emergency Tinder or Campmor's Fire Lighters) in a real survival situation. Make it a practice to carry a waterproof match container supplied with a fresh supply of strike-anywhere matches and fire starters with you at all times in your survival kit. This combination helps make fire starting in cold, wet, dark conditions much quicker and easier. Make sure you replace the matches every six months or so as they deteriorate over several months and become useless.

It might sound silly, but make sure you practice using them, too, and not just on nice days to be outside. Far too many people think that with matches or a cigarette lighter they can build a fire. I know a seasoned search and rescue official who tells me that each year he helps find many lost or stranded outdoorsmen who are cold and without a fire. They had matches or a lighter but exhausted them just trying to get a fire started. Seldom do we get lost or stranded in ideal weather. The survival situation is often, in part, caused by bad weather. That requires building a fire in wet, windy, cold conditions that make it difficult at best. Only people well trained in fire building can pull it off.

Leave primitive fire starting techniques to the experts. Use matches and a fire starter for survival purposes.

Take the time to learn an old Boy Scout skill—build a fire with one match in a rainstorm. It's much tougher than many think.

In a tepee fire, the tinder and kindling is arranged in a conical shape for quick ignition.

A pyramid or log-cabin fire will burn downward requiring less attention at night.

Steps to Building a Fire

Understand that you don't just start a fire, you build it. There are five things you need to build a fire successfully:

1. You must have oxygen, since burning is nothing more than rapid oxidation.

2. You must have a source of heat, your matches.

3. You must have tinder to catch the flame of the match and start the fire. Your prepackaged fire starter is a good start. Add to that natural tinder such as a bird's nest, bark

from a birch tree, cedar bark, down from thistle, pinesap splinters or dry grass. Even fine steel wool has been used as tinder when the strands are pulled apart loosely.

4. You will need small sticks and twigs to catch the fire from the tinder, thus making it hotter.

5. You will need dry, dead fuel wood and a lot more of it than you will think. Dry, dead wood can be hard to find in wet weather, but some can usually be found on the lower limbs of evergreen trees, standing dead timber or splitting wet logs or large limbs and getting to their dry wood interiors.

Building a fire in the first attempt requires practice and thought. Many try to add large pieces of wood too quickly. Others try to pile on so much wood that the flame gets too little oxygen to burn. Still others do not gather up the different sizes of wood necessary to build a

fire in advance, and the fire goes out while they are running around trying to find the tinder, small sticks and fuel wood necessary.

Birch bark makes good tinder for getting a fire going.

If you expect search planes, or are in a position so that ground searchers might see your fire or smoke, keep plenty of kindling and fuel wood on hand to get a fire going again quickly for signaling. Better yet, work at keeping your fire going at all times so you don't have to start another one from scratch. Also, during the day, keep some green or wet leaves or conifer boughs on hand to create signal smoke quickly.

Can you really build a fire with one match when you are cold, shaking, wet, tired and scared? Again, practice at home! This is the time to master the art, not when it really counts.

Fire can be used for light, to harden a wooden spear, warmth, to keep away insects, as a signal, to boil drinking water and many other purposes.

Sleeping Warm

Sleeping warm and comfortably cannot be emphasized enough in a survival emergency. You need a lot of energy for the tasks at hand, and the mind needs to be sharper than during your normal day-to-day life as the decisions you make determine your well-being and the outcome of your situation.

The MPI Space bag you carry in your survival kit will help keep you warm on a cold night.

The combination of a lean-to with a reflector fire to direct heat into the shelter makes a comfortable sleeping shelter.

If you have a tube tent and MPI Space bag in your survival kit, and get the tube tent up so that you can get into the bag before you get wet, then chances are good you will sleep warm. How well you clean the tube tent site will determine how comfortably you sleep. Taking a few minutes to remove stones, sticks, etc., and laying down a bed of dry leaves can make the difference between a long, miserable night and a comfortable, warm night of sleep.

But what about a night spent without the aid of a tube tent or Space bag? In this case there are several options, depending upon the terrain where you determine to camp. The first rule is to get into a shelter of some type that can give you protection from the rain, snow or wind. If this shelter makes it easier for you to get a fire going, so much the better. Your chances of actually getting some sleep improve when you can stay warm. Be sure to gather three times as much wood as you think you will need, as it will probably take that much to keep the fire going all night. It is difficult to keep the body warm or to get enough sleep when you must make two or three trips out into the cold darkness to gather wood.

The ideal sleeping shelter, aside from the tube tent/Space bag combination, is the lean-to with its back to the wind and a reflector fire directing heat into the shelter. Using a sheet of aluminum foil, a wall of green limbs, rocks, etc., as a reflector, the all-night fire can keep a lean-to reasonably warm as long as there is enough wood. As the fire begins to die, simply toss on enough wood to keep it going another few hours.

When rain or snow is not a threat, a reflector fire directing heat toward a large rock or dirt bank that is also blocking the wind can make for a nice place to sleep. The heat is reflected toward the rock or bank and back onto you while you sleep. You have heat from two sides.

The reflector fire is one of the best fires for keeping warm in very cold weather.

You can build a fire on the spot you plan to sleep on and let it warm the earth for a few hours, then rack the fire away to a new spot and sleep on the warm earth. If you have a means of digging, you can also dig a shallow hole where you plan to lie, shovel in a bed of hot ashes and cover them up with a layer of soil. Make sure to cover all of the ashes and check to ensure you have enough soil over them before simply lying down. You don't want to have a too-hot or too-cold bed. Using coals and ashes is an energy-consuming means of having a warm bed.

Some experienced backwoodsmen heat a number of flat rocks and place them on the ground. Next they place a thick layer of precut evergreen boughs over the rocks and sleep on them. Again, this type of warm sleeping requires a lot of energy and experience.

If you don't have a Space bag, sleeping bag or blanket, you can use dry dead grass, leaves or evergreen boughs to provide some protection from the cold. Remember that insulation is dead air space and anything that will create dead air space will help keep you warm. The rain suit can offer a lot of warmth when sleeping due to its ability to stop the wind from hitting your skin. Also, stuffing dead, dry grass or leaves inside the rain suit can make it into a makeshift sleeping bag. Be resourceful.

Here are some other tips to getting a good night's sleep:

1. Take the time to make the bed site as level and soft as possible.

2. Be sure to use every windbreak available.

3. Gather three times as much wood as you think you need.

4. Eat sweets, if you have them, just before bedtime to boost your metabolism.

5. Do not lie awake the first night expecting searchers every minute; you will hear them if they get close and you will need to be rested the next day.

6. At night, due to your situation, your senses will be acutely aware and you will hear every noise. Remember, there is nothing out there that will hurt you. If something awakens you, make sure it is not searchers; if so, have your whistle available, and then go back to sleep.

7. When sleeping with your clothes on, keep everything loose, including boots. The better circulation you have, the warmer you will sleep. Also, this permits moisture to evaporate.

You can bet that even in the best of circumstances you are not going to sleep in the survival camp as well as you do at home, but with a little care you can get some sleep and that rest is most important to your getting found.

10. INSECTS

Dealing with Insects

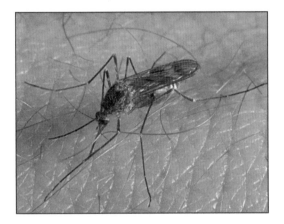

Few things can ruin an outdoor adventure faster than hordes of mosquitoes and/or black flies. In

Mosquitoes are encountered throughout a wide range of North American habitats.

large numbers, they have been known to bring armies to a halt, stampede animals and turn countless camping, fishing and hunting trips into horror stories. In a stranded or lost emergency they can become very dangerous. Even in cold areas, a sudden warm snap can bring the pests out in numbers.

Mosquitoes

Of the more than 1,600 varieties of mosquitoes, 120 are found in North America. Many of these are known to transmit such diseases as West Nile virus, encephalitis and dengue fever. Their bites alone, in high numbers, are very dangerous.

To deal with these flying pests, we need to know more about them. Mosquitoes mature in standing water. It is the female mosquito that causes us grief, as she needs a high-protein meal before she is able to lay her eggs. Physiological restrictions make it impossible for her to eat anything that is not in liquid form, and the handiest liquid, high-protein meal available to her is blood. The male mosquito is a vegetarian and feeds on plant and fruit nectar.

Sensors, which are attracted to warm, moist animals, help the female mosquito locate a meal. The generally accepted theory in the scientific community is that the mosquito finds its victim by identifying and following carbon dioxide and lactic acid in the air. Lactic acid is produced by muscle movement, and carbon dioxide is given off when we breathe.

Once she finds a victim, a female mosquito penetrates the victim's skin with a hollow, flexible snout, called a proboscis, and feeds. The itch and local swelling around the "bite" is an allergic reaction to the mosquito's saliva, which contains an anticoagulant to facilitate the flow of blood.

Black Flies

For those who have been bitten by black flies, the bite is a form of torture. These small, humpbacked flies certainly have few equals when it comes to inflicting pain. Of the more than 300 varieties of black flies in the world, North America has been cursed with at least 50.

Some species of adult black flies are fierce biters while others cause a nuisance by swarming around exposed skin areas.

Unlike the mosquito, the black fly thrives in running water. Rapidly flowing streams are preferred breeding places. Once able to fly, the female, which feeds by day, is ready for a meal in order to carry out her task of reproduction.

Like the mosquito, the black fly is found over much of North America, but its largest concentrations are in the woodlands of Canada and in the northern part of the United States. This insect is abundant throughout late spring and summer, with May and June being the worst months in many areas.

The vicious bite of the black fly is caused by broad blades found in the mouth parts of the fly. These blades make relatively large wounds, which continue to bleed after the fly has fed and gone. Often the bite goes unnoticed until a trickle of blood is felt or seen. Black fly saliva may be toxic, causing pain and itching and sometimes nervous and intestinal disorders.

Not as much is known about the black fly as about the mosquito, so we can't say what actually draws this insect to its target. But it is thought that the female black fly detects the carbon dioxide given off by the skin and then follows the convection currents of warm, moist air that the host produces.

Anyone who plans to venture into the backcountry should always carry a good supply of chemical insect repellent, even if the trip is a short one. Repellent should always be included in a survival kit as it is the most effective mosquito and black fly deterrent. Repellents work by confusing the flying critter and discouraging it from feeding on the victim.

The development of effective repellents was slow, and it wasn't until the late 1950s that a repellent compound was developed that started providing the desired results. It was N, N-diethyl-meta-toluamide and was given the

shorter name DEET. This new compound was used by the military in the jungles of Vietnam at a 75 percent concentration. Today it is still the best single ingredient insect repellent. No one is sure why DEET works so well, but scientists think that it acts as an olfactory irritant for insects, confusing their sensors and making target identification difficult.

A mosquito can sense carbon dioxide and lactic acid, chemicals exuded by mammals, up to 100 feet away.

The percentage of DEET in an insect repellent can determine how long the product will provide protection. If the insect repellent you purchase has 10 to 15 percent DEET, you can expect approximately four hours of protection;

from 20 to 50 percent, approximately six hours; 50 to 75 percent, approximately eight hours; and 75 to 100 percent, a full day of protection. This varies from person to person, but it is a good rule of thumb to go by.

Outdoorsmen today are blessed with a number of excellent insect repellents to choose from at the drug- or sporting goods store. I carry Ben's Tick and Insect Repellent single-use pouches in my survival kit. They take up little space and work well. When using any of these chemical repellents, you should follow some simple guidelines:

1. Read all label directions carefully.

2. When using aerosol repellents, always keep spray opening aimed away from your face, and avoid spraying while smoking or close to fire.

3. For the best protection, repellent should be applied to all exposed skin except your eyes, lips and broken areas of skin.

4. Avoid repellent contact with outdoor equipment and clothing made of Spandex, rayon, acrylics or plastics. It can dissolve monofilament fishing line, gunstock finishes and plastic lenses in glasses.

5. Reapply repellent after swimming or perspiring heavily, since water or perspiration will weaken a repellent's effectiveness.

Repellents alone will not give you total protection from mosquitoes and black flies in areas of heavy infestations. A head net may be well worth the bother at certain times.

In bug country, you should always wear a long-sleeved shirt and trousers. Apply a repellent containing an appropriate percentage of DEET to the clothing as well as to your exposed skin. To keep the pests from invading the openings of your clothing, use short lengths of cord to tie down your shirtsleeves and trouser legs.

When using a repellent, the trick is to apply enough to get complete coverage. According to experts, it takes approximately five seconds of spray time to cover the wrist to the elbow. Most people try to do it in less than one second.

In a survival situation during warm weather, pick a campsite with insect control in mind. Stay away from pools of stagnant water. Pick sites located on high breezy points or at least in the open where you can take advantage of any breeze that may help keep the insects away.

When There Is No Repellent

There are often occasions where the lost or stranded person either has run out of repellent or has none and the flying pests are out in vast numbers. When this happens, the first thing to do is to cover up all exposed skin areas. Tuck trouser legs into boots. Button sleeves tight around the wrist. Pull up shirt and coat collars to protect the neck. Put on a hat and gloves. In short, give the biting critters as small a target as possible.

Next, build a smoky fire near your shelter; and at a time like this, the smokier the better. Lie down and put your face near the ground to keep your eyes and nose as free of the smoke as possible. While this may be irritating, it is better than being fed on by flying pests. In severe conditions, build two fires and sit in the middle. There is no good substitute for carrying insect repellent in your survival kit.

Ticks

While ticks are a potential long-term health threat

North American tick species include the American dog tick, the lone star tick, and the blacklegged or deer tick.

with diseases such as Lyme disease or Rocky Mountain spotted fever, they do not pose the immediate threat that large numbers of flying pests do. Ticks should be avoided; and when found on the body, removed.

The recommended way to remove an embedded tick is to use tweezers and gently but firmly pull the tick straight out. Avoid jerking or twisting the tick, as the head may remain embedded. After removing the tick, wash the bite area with soap and water and apply an antiseptic if you can.

Making Water Safe
for Drinking

No longer can you trust the water found in backcountry, no matter how remote or how clean the water appears. Treat all water
before drinking.

There once was a time when it would have been unnecessary to include a chapter in this book on how to make water found in the backcountry safe for drinking, but those days are gone. Today there are few areas left where one can trust the quality of the water and be safe in doing so. Therefore, it behooves every backcountry traveler to learn the skill of making water safe for drinking, especially those who might possibly face a survival emergency.

Survival is a stressful period in a person's life, and the need for pure drinking water is important. The body is approximately 75 percent water, and the intake and output of liquids are necessary for normal functions of the vital organs.

Daily water requirements, a minimum of two quarts, help maintain proper balance and efficiency within the system of the body. During cold weather, breathing alone releases a lot of moisture from the body. Perspiration also releases moisture. Any lower intake of water results in gradual dehydration. Losing water to the extent of 2.5 percent of body weight, or approximately one and one-half quarts of body water, will reduce your body's operational efficiency 25 percent. This loss could be deadly in a survival emergency.

There are many myths about water purifying itself in the outdoors. One popular theory is that water, swiftly running over, around and through rocks purifies itself. Do not believe it. This is not a valid hypothesis. Another myth claims that if clear water sits in the sun for an hour, the germs are killed. Again, this is untrue. Nature produces clean water, but once it becomes unclean, rarely does nature clean it again. It is your responsibility to treat questionable water.

Never trust water from an unknown source. If you do not know the source of your water supply, do not trust it. Some of the diseases you may contract by drinking impure water include dysentery, Giardia, cholera and typhoid. The best way to be assured of having safe water is to carry enough with you to use for drinking. However, in an unexpected survival situation of several days, this is not always possible. It is on these types of emergencies that water treatment knowledge is a must. Here are several methods for treating questionable water:

Boiling Water — One of the best methods for treating water is the boiling method.

Boiling water for 10 minutes will produce germ-free water for drinking or cooking. Since boiling leaves water with a flat taste, you should

pour it back and
forth between two
containers several
times once it has
cooled. This aerates
it, giving back its
natural taste. A ves-
sel for boiling water
can be formed from
the aluminum foil in
your survival kit.

Commercial
Tablets — Drug
stores and outfitter
stores usually have
halazone tablets or
Potable Aqua tablets for the treatment of
water. A bottle of the tablets fits nicely in the
individual survival kit. Both do an excellent job.
Halazone tablets have been used successfully
for years. Add two tablets to a quart of water
and follow with a 30-minute wait. The newer
product, Potable Aqua, requires one tablet to a
quart of water, capping loosely to allow a little
leakage. Wait three minutes and shake thor-
oughly. Wait 10 minutes before drinking. If the
water is very cold or contains rotten leaves or
silt, use two tablets and wait 20 minutes before
drinking. You can use the gallon resealable plastic bag in which your survival items are packed

Water treatment tablets such as
Potable Aqua should be in all survival kits.

for a water container. Also, the plastic bag in which the tube tent is packed makes a good water container.

Clorox Treatment — Clorox, the washing bleach that makes clothes sparkling white, is another excellent water treatment. To each quart of questionable water add 10 drops of pure Clorox. If for some reason the water is cloudy, add 20 drops. Next shake the water vigorously and let it sit for 30 minutes. There should be a slight chlorine odor and taste if the water is properly treated. If not, add another 10 drops of Clorox and let the water stand for an additional 15 minutes.

Iodine Treatment — While iodine is no longer used in some of the newer first-aid kits, it is still in older kits and makes a good water treatment. Simply add five drops of iodine to one quart of clear water and 10 drops to cloudy water. Let water stand for 30 minutes before drinking.

At this point I should point out that anytime you are treating water in a canteen, jug or other type of container, you should be sure to rinse the cap, spout, screw threads, lid, etc., with some of the treated water. You do not want to miss treating any surface that may come in contact with your mouth or the water you are drinking.

Water Filtering Devices — There are a number of compact water filtration units, such as Pur, Katadyn and MSR that can give the back-country traveler safe water. They have been proven to filter out Giardia and other harmful threats and the unit fits into a pack easily.

Getting Water Under Extreme Cold Conditions — Anytime you are traveling under frigid conditions, you should take along a reliable backpack stove. Once you have the stove going, look for sources of water.

Whenever possible, melt ice for water rather than snow. You get more water for the volume with less heat and time.

Water filtering devices are good for making water safe to drink. If there is room, they are a good item to have in your daypack.

Remember, snow is seventeen parts air and one part water. If you melt snow by heating, put in a little at a time and compress it, or the pot will burn. If water is available, put a little in the bottom of the pot and add snow gradually.

Glacial ice gives roughly twice the water per fuel unit in half the time that snow does when melted. In addition, snow more often contains dirt, soot and animal and human contaminants. Do not try to eat ice or snow. A day or two of taking water in this manner produces a swollen, raw mucous membrane in the mouth, which may become painful enough to prevent eating or drinking until the inflammation subsides. Dogs eat snow and get away with it; humans cannot. Once you have water, give it the boiling treatment.

Collecting Rain and Dew for Drinking Water — When surface water is scarce, dew can be collected off plant leaves, vehicle surfaces, tube tent surface, etc., with a cloth and squeezed into a vessel. Some dew can be collected on the underside of a plastic sheet spread on the ground during the night.

If it rains, collect water by funneling runoff into your gallon plastic bag. A rain suit can be used to catch rain by digging a hole in the ground and lining it with the jacket. This assumes, of course, that you will stay dry in your tube tent or shelter.

Getting Sediment Out of Water — If clear water is not available, take the following steps:

1. Filter the water to be treated through a clean handkerchief or similar fabric.

2. Let the filtered water stand until any remaining sediment has settled to the bottom.

3. Pour off the clear water into the vessel which you plan to treat it in, and then treat the water.

Food —
Not a Necessity

Every time the subject of survival is brought up, the first discussions usually revolve around edible wild foods and how to procure them. We are obsessed with eating. It has been proven many times that most of us can go without eating several weeks, if necessary, and not die. Most of us carry around an abundance of fat that could keep us alive for a long period of time. For this reason, and the fact this book was written for the most likely survival scenario of spending less than 72 hours in the woods, we will not cover the many edible wild plants and animals that are available in North America.

Edible Wild Plants

For those who think they cannot go for three days without eating three meals a day, I would suggest they read and study the many survival and other books that describe and show detailed photos of the approximately 2,000 edible wild plants and 700 toxic wild plants found in North America. Distinguishing one from the other requires a lot of field experience during all four seasons. A little book like this cannot scratch the surface on this subject.

We can live for weeks without food to eat. Avoid the temptation of eating wild foods such as insects unless you are well trained in identification of wild foods.

Wild Plant Edibility Test

If for some reason you are in a situation where there are wild plants you think you must eat but don't know which ones are edible, the U.S. Air Force Edibility Test may be of some help:

1. Never use mushrooms or fungi.

2. Poisonous plant life means all parts, including flowers, can be toxic. Use caution with plants having these characteristics:

    > Milky or discolored sap
    > Spines or fine hairs
    > Bitter or soapy taste
    > Beans or bulbs
    > White or red berries
    > Shiny leaves
    > Umbrella flowers

3. Take a small mouthful and chew it. Wait five minutes for any effects such as burning, stinging, or numbing.

4. If there is none, swallow and wait eight hours for any effects such as diarrhea, cramps, pains, numbing, vomiting, etc.

5. If there is none, repeat the process, using a handful of the plant, and wait another eight hours for ill effects.

6. If none, the plant is considered safe to eat.

Keep in mind that any new or strange food should be eaten with restraint until the body system has become accustomed to it. Also, don't expect wild plants to taste good; many don't and others are almost tasteless. It takes some adjustment to get your stomach to accept a diet of wild plants.

Some other things you need to know about wild plants:

1. Plants you see animals eating may be toxic to man. Deer love poison ivy.

2. Plants that may be edible in one stage of its growth cycle may not be edible in others, such as pokeweed.

3. Plants that contain one edible part may be inedible on other parts, such as the wild plum.

Edible Wild Animals

If the survivor really must resort to wild foods in order not to starve to death, then wild animals may be a better choice. That is if he has hunting and trapping skills. North America has a good population of wild animals, both large and small, that are edible. The trick is that you first must get them before you can cook them. Even the Lewis and Clark expedition members, at one point, almost starved to death due to not killing any game to eat and had to depend upon roots.

Depending upon the time of year and where you are geographically, there is some form of animal that you can eat if you can catch or kill it. Insects and small aquatic animals may be the easiest to gather and highest in protein, but what if it is winter? There may be an abundance of larger animals; but if you lack the skills necessary to kill them, you could go hungry. And remember, animals are often hard to find even by the most skilled hunters. Provided you can kill them, wild animals are a good source of food and may be cooked over the survival fire with ease. Just don't expect them to taste like home cooking.

Survival food is not an important need for short term. Shelter and signaling are. Accept the fact that the last thing you should concern yourself with is the procurement of food. If you have filed a trip plan with a responsible person and just as soon as you knew you were in trouble you stopped, you will be rescued long before your hunger pains become serious. Think of this experience as the beginning of that diet you have been considering.

It takes a lot of experience to be an effective gatherer of wild foods. You will not need those skills for short-term survival. This is a good time to start your diet.

13. HYPOTHERMIA

Avoid Hypothermia

Hypothermia sneaks up on its victim. Cool weather, wind and wet clothing lead to hypothermia.

Hypothermia, a lowering of the core temperature of the body, can be a killer. It can strike in any season and in almost any climate. All that is needed is a mild air temperature—30 to 50°F, wetness, rain, sweat, a creek dunking, a slight wind and a tired person.

Hypothermia attacks a person in two steps. The first is when your body begins to lose heat faster than it produces it. At this point, you are aware of feeling cold, and the shivering begins.

The second step is when the cold reaches the brain, depriving you of good judgment. It is at this point that confusion will take over decision making. This is the reason almost no one recognizes that he or she has hypothermia. In the second step, your internal temperature slides downward. Without treatment, this slide leads to stupor, collapse and death. Each year many people become lost due to confusion brought on by early stages of hypothermia.

There are several ways to avoid hypothermia:

1. Stay dry. When clothing gets wet it may lose 90 percent of its insulating value. Even sweating can bring on hypothermia.

2. Beware of the wind chill. A slight breeze carries heat away from bare skin faster

than still air. It turns wet clothing into a refrigerator due to evaporation.

3. Understand cold. Most hypothermia cases develop in air temperatures that are considered mild, wind chill temperatures in the 40s and 50s. Most people do not believe such temperatures can be dangerous.

4. Terminate exposure. When you cannot stay warm and dry in existing weather conditions, either get a fire going at a natural shelter out of the wind or set up your tube tent and get into the emergency bag. Get out of the wind and dampness, and get warm, as fast as possible.

5. Never ignore shivering. Persistent or violent shivering is clear warning that you are in the early stages of hypothermia.

When hypothermia symptoms are noticed, treatment should begin immediately. First get the victim out of the weather and remove his wet clothing. If the victim is only mildly impaired, give him warm drinks and get him into dry clothing and a tube tent and emergency bag.

Wind Chill Chart

ESTIMATED WIND IN MPH	ACTUAL THERMOMETER READING (F)											
	50	40	30	20	10	00	-10	-20	-30	-40	-50	-60
	EQUIVALENT TEMPERATURE (F)											
CALM	50	40	30	20	10	00	-10	-20	-30	-40	-50	-60
5	48	37	27	16	6	-5	-15	-26	-36	-47	-57	-68
10	40	28	16	4	-9	-21	-33	-46	-58	-70	-83	-95
15	36	22	9	-5	-18	-36	-45	-58	-72	-85	-99	-112
20	32	13	4	-10	-25	-39	-53	-67	-82	-96	-110	-124
25	50	16	0	-15	-29	-44	-59	-74	-88	-104	-118	-133
30	28	13	-2	-18	-33	-48	-63	-79	-94	-109	-125	-140
35	27	11	-4	-20	-35	-49	-67	-82	-99	-113	-129	-145
40	26	10	-6	-21	-37	-53	-69	-85	-100	-116	-132	-148
(WIND SPEEDS GREATER THAN 40 MPH HAVE LITTLE ADDITIONAL EFFECT)	LITTLE DANGER (FOR PROPERLY CLOTHED PERSON)		INCREASING DANGER		GREAT DANGER							
			DANGER OF FREEZING EXPOSED FLESH									

If the victim is semiconscious or worse, he does not have the capability of regaining his body temperature without outside help. Keep him awake, give him warm drinks and, if possible, get him into a warm bath. If possible, strip the victim and put him into an emergency bag with another person. Skin-to-skin contact is an effective treatment.

Initial symptoms of hypothermia, the loss of core body temperature, include mood changes, lassitude, irritability and poor judgment.

As the body core temperature drops, here is how hypothermia affects you:

98.6° to 96°
Uncontrolled shivering, ability to perform complex tasks impaired.

95° to 91°
Violent shivering, difficulty in speaking.

90° to 86°
Shivering decreases, muscles begin to stiffen—lose coordination. Mind becomes dull; in some cases, amnesia occurs.

85° to 81°
Victim becomes irrational, drifts into stupor. Pulse and respiration are slowed. Muscular rigidity continues.

80° to 78°
Unconsciousness. Reflexes cease to function and heartbeat becomes erratic.

Below 78°
Total failure of cardiac and respiration systems. Death occurs.

In a survival situation, every effort should be made to avoid hypothermia. That means getting a warm camp set up before you get wet and cold. Don't put off getting a survival camp established. Delay can be deadly.

Avoid hypothermia at all cost!

Dealing with Fear

Panic, a state of sudden uncontrollable fear or anxiety, results in irrational behavior and poorly considered hasty decisions.

Most people think, "Survival training is something I won't need." But each year, scores of hunters and other outdoor enthusiasts find themselves suddenly lost or stranded in North America's backcountry, often not too far from home.

One of the first reactions to being lost or stranded is fear. It is fear that causes many people to panic soon after they realize that they are in a potential survival situation. It is fear that makes people run and discard their equipment.

Here is what research has shown us that most people fear in a survival situation:

Ridicule or Embarrassment — Those I have interviewed soon after rescue said this was the first fear they experienced. This is especially a major fear of experienced outdoorsmen who want to maintain their "Daniel Boone" image. Put ego aside and get into survival mode.

Punishment — It is this fear that causes many lost children and senior citizens to hide soon after they realize they are lost. Coupled with this concern is the fear of being late. Most of us live our daily lives as slaves to a clock, and when we aren't where we are supposed to be, when we are supposed to be there, we face some form of punishment. This fear of punishment is present in every survival situation.

Being Alone — Many people, including outdoorsmen, have never been truly alone. To them this is a strange and suddenly frightening experience. I once led a small search team for an experienced worldwide hunter. While he was only lost for a few hours, this man was in shock, as he had never been alone except in a room or other such circumstance. The few hours he spent lost, alone, caused him to end his hunting career.

Animals — Many people have hidden fears of wild animals and sounds in the woods. The fear of wild animals is mentioned by many formerly lost or stranded people, especially children. Most people forget under the stress of survival that wild animals prefer to avoid people and, with a few rare exceptions, wild animals of North America don't attack people.

Discomfort — We are so accustomed to comfort that the idea that we may get cold, hungry, thirsty, have to sleep on the hard ground, etc., can cause people to panic. In order to survive, you must accept some discomfort and remember that this short period of discomfort is necessary for you to live the rest of your life. This should motivate you to try hard to build a comfortable survival camp while awaiting rescue. Discomfort can be tolerated until help arrives.

The Unknown — We all live in a fairly predictable day-to-day world. We know daily, hourly, what we can expect to happen. When we find ourselves suddenly in a survival situation, this comfort of knowing is quickly converted into the fear of the unknown—what should I do now, will anyone look for me, will I die? All these unknowns rush through the mind and cloud common sense. This fear is a normal reaction, but the quicker you overcome it and put your survival training to work the better. Mentally accept, "Yes, there are many unknowns, but I can't worry about them now as I have a camp to make and signals to prepare. I am going to have a great adventure story to tell when this is all over."

Darkness — One of the most common fears, even though many will not admit it, is the fear of darkness in the woods. I have seen some otherwise brave men admit, privately, that they fear a dark night in the woods. It always amazes me that these same people are not afraid of a dark street in a large city where danger is always nearby but become almost paralyzed with fear in the woods at night. There is little to hurt anyone in the woods at night, if they stay in one location. To panic and start walking or, worst yet, running in dark woods can lead to serious falls or getting a stick in your eye. There is little in the woods at night that will harm you. Just stay in your survival camp and get a good night's sleep.

Controlling Fear

We all have some, or all, of these fears when we find ourselves in a survival emergency. However, those who get control of their fears quickly and move on with the task of being found are the ones that come out of the situation in good shape. Here is how you can cope and live with fear during your survival experience:

1. Don't run away from fear, admit and accept it as being a normal reaction.

2. Even when you are afraid, act to accomplish those necessities of selecting a campsite, setting up signals, constructing a shelter, getting a fire going and preparing to sleep comfortably. Be enthusiastic.

3. Accept the mindset that "this has happened to me and I am going to make it through in good shape." Hope for the best and be prepared for the worst.

4. Stay busy. Idleness leads to negative thinking and hopelessness.

5. Practice your religion.

6. Keep a positive attitude.

15. WILL TO LIVE

There have been countless numbers of people who were lost or stranded for weeks without food, fire or shelter. When they were found, they were in good shape. On the other hand there have been cases where people were lost just a day or so, and they perished. The difference between these people was that the ones who made it through in good condition did so because they had a strong WILL TO LIVE. They never gave up on the hope of being found. They made the best of a bad situation. They didn't panic. They stayed put. They made the best of the resources at hand; and they had, or quickly developed, a positive mental attitude. In today's terminology, they kept their cool. You have to value life in order to take charge of your mind and the situation in which you find yourself. Give up your value of life and you will not last long.

Once you get over the first shock wave that you are lost or stranded, put a high value on your life and capitalize on your WILL TO LIVE. You will be amazed at what it will get you through.

16. MISSING PERSON

When a Member of Your Group Is Missing

Have you been on an outing when you suddenly realized you were lost or stranded and/or unable to return to camp or your vehicle? If not, get ready, because if you go into the back-country enough, chances are, it will happen eventually. As a wildlife professional, I have spent considerable time looking for missing outdoorsmen. Most of the time, they are simply turned around in the woods and are easily found.

However, some are injured and unable to move, often due to a fall from a tree stand or a slippery rock or log. Once, a guide who worked for me fell into an abandoned well.

Unfortunately, some outdoor enthusiasts are brought out dead as a result of heart attacks, falls or hypothermia. Often the cause of death is brought on by the stress of being lost.

While many outdoor people are learning what to do if they should become lost or stranded, few know what to do if their buddy does not make it back to the car or camp when he is supposed to. Every group, whether it is an outing club or just two friends, should plan ahead for that moment when one of them

Resist the temptation to start a search for a missing person. If professional help is nearby, let them put their experience to work.

is missing. This is just as important whether you are exploring your own back forty or are traveling in a remote wilderness.

It should be a policy that every member of the group let the others know specifically where they are going and when they plan to return. All members of the group should agree to sit tight once they realize they are lost. This should be stressed over and over again. Every member of the group should carry a compass

When you plan to enter a wilderness area, always let someone know where you are going and when you plan to return.

(that they know how to use), a GPS, a map of the area, a cell phone or two-way radio, a belt knife and a survival kit.

Know the medical condition of your companions. If a member of your group has a heart problem, seizures or other medical problem, make sure a buddy hunts with him. An unconscious person needs to be found quickly, but is extremely difficult to find.

Each member of your group needs to know how to locate the nearest conservation officer, forest ranger or sheriff's office. In most counties in the United States, the local sheriff is responsible for search and rescue. In Canada, the local Royal Canadian Mounted Police officer is usually responsible for searches. Everyone should carry the phone numbers of these officials. Delay in getting trained search and rescue help can be deadly.

Always be aware of how your fellow companions are dressed, what type of boots they wear and the state of mind they are in. This information is extremely valuable to search officials.

The most crucial time during a missing-buddy crisis is when you first realize he or she is late coming into camp and you get no answers to your signals. Don't panic. The first rule is to stay calm and THINK. In most cases, lost or stranded situations are merely a sobering two- or three-hour adventure.

Signaling is an important part of the early search, as rescued people often say that while they were lost or stranded they thought no one would bother to look for them. Select a logical point, such as where he was last seen, the logging road or field nearest his "most likely" area, camp or his vehicle if he drove in, and blow an automobile horn or police whistle. Either of these signals is an indication to the missing person that someone is looking for him. If he is nearby, he can walk to the sound. For this reason, it is crucial that the signaling be done from one spot and not done as you move around.

Blow the horn or whistle in bursts of three so that it is obviously a signal and not some unrelated noise. Pause between bursts of three and listen carefully for a reply. If the missing person has a whistle, you may hear a response immediately. If you are getting no response to your initial signaling and feel that your buddy may be in trouble, seek out a forest ranger, conservation officer or sheriff's department official to get trained search and rescue people on the scene as soon as possible. If you leave to obtain professional help, leave someone at the signal point. While one person goes for help, another should always stay to continue signaling and listening if possible.

Attempting to set up your own search is generally a bad idea since most untrained people with the best of intentions usually do more harm than good. They destroy valuable clues and often become lost or hurt themselves. Searching for missing people is a skill best left to those trained to do it.

However, in some specific circumstances, such as when help is hours away or when the tract of

When searching for a lost group member, appoint a group leader to coordinate the search and oversee the best use of resources.

land is not large and it is known almost exactly where the missing person is likely to be, fellow outdoorsmen might conduct a limited search. In those exceptional cases, follow these guidelines:

1. Get the entire group together to plan your search. To help identify clues, find out what each member knows, such as when and where the missing buddy was last seen, did he file a trip plan, what brand of cigarettes he smokes, what type of sole does he have on his boots and their size, where he is most likely hunting and so on.

2. Establish someone in the group as leader of the search, and have everyone do as he says.

3. Leave someone at the original spot to continue signaling.

4. If a specific hunting spot is known, two hunters should begin the search with a thorough examination of the immediate area in case there was a health problem or injury. Take care not to destroy any signs. It is important that only one or two do this, as a larger group will destroy clues that might be helpful if a professional search is needed.

5. Look for signs such as tracks or, in the case of

hunters, blood trail markers for an indication of the missing person's direction of travel.

6. Due to the excitement of the moment, searchers often get lost themselves, so mark the trail you take in so you can follow it out.

7. Consider what sounds the missing person can hear, farm, railroad, highway, mill whistle, etc., and send someone to that location. Rather than sit still, many lost people will try to walk to sounds such as these.

8. If there are roads around the area, a vehicle should patrol these roads regularly, but do not blow the horn as you travel.

9. If there is a long opening in the area such as a railroad, gas line or electric line right-of-way or large fields, have someone watch these areas with binoculars.

10. Plan a signal or specific time for calling off the search. If the missing person has not been found within a short time, turn the search over to professionals.

If you and your outdoor companions have prepared for the day one of you is missing, chances are you will never be faced with a tragedy.

Notes

_____
_____
_____
_____
_____
_____
_____
_____
_____
_____
_____
_____
_____
_____
_____
_____
_____
_____
_____
_____
_____
_____
_____

Notes

Notes

Notes

_____

_____

_____

_____

_____

_____

_____

_____

_____

_____

_____

_____

_____

_____

_____

_____

_____

_____

_____

_____

_____

_____

_____

_____

_____

_____

Notes

Notes

_____
_____
_____
_____
_____
_____
_____
_____
_____
_____
_____
_____
_____
_____
_____
_____
_____
_____
_____
_____
_____
_____
_____
_____

Notes

_____

_____

_____

_____

_____

_____

_____

_____

_____

_____

_____

_____

_____

_____

_____

_____

_____

_____

_____

_____

_____

_____

_____

Notes

_____

_____

_____

_____

_____

_____

_____

_____

_____

_____

_____

_____

_____

_____

_____

_____

_____

_____

_____

_____

_____

_____

_____

_____

Notes

_____
_____
_____
_____
_____
_____
_____
_____
_____
_____
_____
_____
_____
_____
_____
_____
_____
_____
_____
_____
_____
_____
_____
_____
_____

Notes

_____

_____

_____

_____

_____

_____

_____

_____

_____

_____

_____

_____

_____

_____

_____

_____

_____

_____

_____

_____

_____

_____

_____

_____

Notes

_____

_____

_____

_____

_____

_____

_____

_____

_____

_____

_____

_____

_____

_____

_____

_____

_____

_____

_____

_____

_____

_____

_____

Notes

Notes

_____
_____
_____
_____
_____
_____
_____
_____
_____
_____
_____
_____
_____
_____
_____
_____
_____
_____
_____
_____
_____
_____
_____

Notes

Notes